Please READ to ME
Book 4

HARRY THE HOCKEY STICK

Betty "Beattie" Chandorkar

To order additional copies of this book, contact:
Xlibris
1-888-795-4274
www.Xlibris.com
Orders@Xlibris.com

Please READ to ME
Book 4

HARRY THE HOCKEY STICK

Betty "Beattie" Chandorkar

I am a hockey stick–a tall, slim pole with a flat blade at the end. The player holds me by both hands and aims my blade to hit the puck, a little black rubber disc, toward a net at the end playing area. The game is usually played on an ice surface called a rink. The players wear skates and skim over the smooth ice. As they develop great speed, hockey becomes a very fast and dangerous game.

My owner, Jim, looks so huge when he is decked out in his hockey uniform. He wears body pads, gloves, and a helmet with a face guard. I am surprised that he can move about so quickly.

There is a goalie, all cushioned up, who squats in the net to prevent the puck from coming into the cage. The goalie holds a bigger and wider stick and, although he wears skates, he seldom leaves his guard position at the door of the net.

Players treat their sticks in a different way. They may bash us onto the ice to signal to their teammates. They might hit us against other players' legs to trip them out of the way and bang us against other sticks as they try to get the puck.

Life of a hockey stick is short. We can be broken, snapped, and splintered so easily in a game. My young owner, Jim, tapes my handle and the blade so carefully and treats me with respect. I work with him to control the puck and bring it down the ice toward the goal. He also sends it back and forth to his team members who may be able to shoot it past the goalie and score.

The players on the opposite team fight to get the puck and drive me out of Jim's hands. If I land on the ice, I am in a scary position with the sharp skates and clashing sticks all around me.

"Here I am, Jimmy, come and get me! I don't like it here!"

I can be "bladed" and be crushed against the wooden boards at the side of the rink.

The noise of hockey is terribly loud. The crowds yell and scream constantly, and the ice rink echoes these shouts of battle. At one game, I was embarrassed as Jim's mother yelled so hard cheering her son. All Jim could say was, "Ooh, Mother," as he loved her so much. She also took loving care of me as I rested in their home along with skates, elbow and knee pads, and all the extra protection the players need.

Jim and I practice stick handling, shooting to the net, and team skills most nights after school. Our big games are held on Saturdays. We show our skill in so many ways. One time as we were near the net, I begged Jim to help me flip the puck into a small net opening when the goalie was looking the other way . . .

We shot! We scored!

Oh, I love this game!

Hockey, of course, is a winter game, but some boys and girls play road or ball hockey in the warmer weather. This extends the game season and does not require a big ice rink or even the sideboards. Traffic on the public road is a problem as the drivers do have the right of way. This game is open to parents and children who wish to enjoy the sport together. The hockey sticks may be a chipped and twisted bunch with loose tape and sometimes missing parts. The community players make do with old sticks just to get out in the fresh air and play.

One warm and sunny spring, I was given a treat. Jim's mother (the noisy one) picked me up and sawed off my chipped and broken blade. She hammered me down into the ground with a big hammer, and I now stand to support a bush in the garden. I am being useful, and the pretty flowers grow at my feet.

I look out over the green lawn and down the sandy hill to the water's edge of the St. Lawrence River. Huge freighter ships sail up and down this famous waterway. To the south, we see the shores of the United States!

Along the river and toward the Great Lakes are the Thousand Islands! I wonder if anyone has ever counted them? I can see three or four islands from where I stand.

During the winter, you would think that I would be lonely standing in a garden overlooking snow and the icy river. But I am not alone. Jim's friends and family all love the winter activities, and I enjoy seeing them play around me.

I know I will not play hockey again, but just below on the river ice, five or six little fellows are shooting a puck and skating madly around the rink they had just cleared of snow.

Jim and his older friends are sliding down the high cliff that once was the riverbank. This hill is too steep for sleds, and the trees and bushes have not been cleared for toboggans and skis. The boys slide on sheets of cardboard and have to twist and turn to miss being crushed by the dangers. The old name for this game is bum sliding!

Jim's younger sister and her friend are lying down, swinging their arms and legs to make angels in the snow. His little brother is building snowmen on the level area near the driveway.

As friends and neighbours are enjoying their winter games, parents get involved. There is Jim's father at the barbecue cooking up a storm, and the ladies are busy getting dishes and sweets ready for a big neighborhood feast.

Now you see why I am not lonely. I stand and watch Jim and his family and friends having great fun in the winter weather.

Now that summer is coming, I look for special company. The thorny little bush that I am holding is growing taller and will soon produce a pretty green bud. Yes, that bud is opening up and displays a beautiful yellow flower–*a yellow rose for friendship*! I hug its stem, and the blossom waves over my head–a glorious, sweet-smelling yellow rose!

What a wonderful way to spend my retirement!

ACTIVITIES

1. Players are always repairing their hockey sticks because they get chipped and broken easily. How do they tape the blade and the handle?.

2. Skating and stick-handling skills. How are they practiced?

3. St. Lawrence River and the Great Lakes waterway open shipping nearly halfway across Canada.

a. Study maps to show the route.
b. Mark the important port cities along this route.
c. Mark the canals and "locks" that permit ships to sail through this amazing system.

d. Don't forget Niagara Falls.

4. There are boat tours in and around some of the Thousand Islands. The Ivy Lea observation tower overlooks some of these lovely areas.

5. Name some of the Olympic winter sports that Canadians excel in.

6. What food would be served at a winter barbecue at Jim's home?

7. The Hockey Hall of Fame in Toronto is open to visitors. The Stanley Cup is on display there.

8. Hockey cards are great to collect and share. They display players, uniforms, and histories.

Printed in the United States
By Bookmasters